Date: 10/26/20

TOOLS FOR CAREGIVERS

- **ATOS:** 0.6
- **GRL:** C
- **WORD COUNT:** 26

- **CURRICULUM CONNECTIONS:** animals

Skills to Teach

- **HIGH-FREQUENCY WORDS:** at, is, let's, look, this
- **CONTENT WORDS:** animal, digs, feels, long, noses, short, sniffs, sprays
- **PUNCTUATION:** exclamation points, periods
- **WORD STUDY:** long /a/, spelled ay (sprays); long /e/, spelled ee (feels); long /o/, spelled o (short); multisyllable word (animal); /oo/, spelled oo (look)
- **TEXT TYPE:** information report

Before Reading Activities

- Read the title and give a simple statement of the main idea.
- Have students "walk" though the book and talk about what they see in the pictures.
- Introduce new vocabulary by having students predict the first letter and locate the word in the text.
- Discuss any unfamiliar concepts that are in the text.

After Reading Activities

We use our noses to smell. But some animals use their noses for much more! Explain to readers that moles live underground and use their noses to feel their way around because their eyesight is so poor. Elephants use their trucks to spray water on themselves. They use them to eat, too! What nose did the readers find the most interesting? Why?

Tadpole Books are published by Jump!, 5357 Penn Avenue South, Minneapolis, MN 55419, www.jumplibrary.com

Copyright ©2020 Jump. International copyright reserved in all countries. No part of this book may be reproduced in any form without written permission from the publisher.

Editor: Jenna Trnka **Designer:** Molly Ballanger

Photo Credits: Soranome/Shutterstock, cover; Utekhina Anna/Shutterstock, 1; uzuri/Shutterstock, 3; studio22comua, 2mr, 4–5; aloha_17/iStock, 2ml, 6–7; Eric Isselee/Shutterstock, 2bl, 8–9; ER Degginger/Science Source, 2tr, 10–11; Juhku/Shutterstock, 2tl, 12–13; Lek_charoen/Shutterstock, 2br, 14–15; yevgeniy11/Shutterstock, 16.

Library of Congress Cataloging-in-Publication Data
Names: Gleisner, Jenna Lee, author.
Title: Noses / by Jenna Lee Gleisner.
Description: Tadpole edition. | Minneapolis, MN: Jump!, Inc., (2020) | Series: Animal part smarts | Audience: Age 3–6. | Includes index.
Identifiers: LCCN 2018042928 (print) | LCCN 2018043972 (ebook) | ISBN 9781641287043 (ebook) | ISBN 9781641287029 (hardcover : alk. paper) | ISBN 9781641287036 (paperback)
Subjects: LCSH: Nose—Juvenile literature.
Classification: LCC QL947 (ebook) | LCC QL947 .G54 2020 (print) | DDC 599.14/4—dc23
LC record available at https://lccn.loc.gov/2018042928

NOSES

by Jenna Lee Gleisner

TABLE OF CONTENTS

tadpole books

WORDS TO KNOW

digs

feels

long

short

sniffs

sprays

NOSES

nose

Let's look at animal noses!

nose

This nose is short.

This nose is long.

This nose sniffs.

nose

This nose feels.

This nose digs!

This nose sprays!

LET'S REVIEW!

What do you notice about these noses?

INDEX